Dinan, Town of Art and His

text Claude Marcel-Rouault
photography Gwenaël Saliou
translation id2m

Cover page.
Rue du Petit-Fort.

Back cover.
The river Rance between Dinan and Lanvallay.

Top, left to right.
Close-up of a capital on St. Saviour's Basilica.

View of Dinan harbour.

The keep.

Opposite.
Rue du Jerzual.

"I love Dinan and the river Rance. The buildings in Rue du Jerzual, from the old harbour to the town square at the top, form a perfect ensemble. The river is magnificent.
Upstream, it becomes calm and serene like the Thames, lined with silver birches and poplars."
Thomas Edward Lawrence,
alias Lawrence of Arabia,
in a letter to his mother in 1907.

Editions OUEST-FRANCE

Introduction

The best view of Dinan can be enjoyed as you approach the town from Lanvallay on the other side of the viaduct, with the old bridge far below. Perched on its rocky outcrop and surrounded by ramparts, the upper part of the town overlooks the peaceful old harbour. Many an artist, enchanted by this view, has set up their easel on the riverbank to depict this town, where each stone is a page of history and the land meets the water's edge.

Dinan started to prosper from the 11th century onwards. The upper town was fortified while, down below, a harbour was built along the river Rance, connecting inland Brittany to the sea. The work of traders and craftsmen added to the town's prosperity.

During the War of Succession, the people of Dinan who took sides with Charles de Blois were besieged by the English on two occasions, once in 1344 and again

2.

1.

3.

in 1364. The latter siege became famous when, in fulfilment of his wife Tiphaine's predictions, the native Bertrand Du Guesclin defeated Sir Thomas Canterbury in a duel. In 1598, during the League, Dinan fought alongside Henri IV. The establishment of enduring peace attracted religious orders to the town which set up monasteries inside its ramparts. During the Counter-Reformation, which followed the Council of Trent, the town was marked by the arrival of Dominican monks and Ursuline nuns. By the 18th century, Dinan was a wealthy town and many mansions were built in and around its mediaeval centre. In the 19th century, cloth and leather manufacturers, fairs and markets ensured the continuing prosperity of Dinan and its residents. In 1879, the arrival of the railway opened up the way for the town's first tourists. Dinan has proudly borne the "Town of Art and History" title since 1984.

1.
The ramparts, St. Saviour's Basilica and the belfry.

2.
The river Rance's peaceful banks.
(Cartopole de Baud)

3.
The old bridge and Dinan harbour.

1.
The keep viewed from the south.

2.
Jerzual Gate.

3.
The keep and its drawbridge viewed from the west.

4.
St. Louis Gate.

5.
St. Catherine's Tower.

The ramparts

The 1065 siege of Dinan by the Normans is illustrated on the famous Bayeux tapestry. A feudal mound, keep and ditches are depicted, testifying to the town's strategic position. However, it was not until 1283, the year that Dinan became a ducal city, that actual fortifications were built around the town.

During the second half of the 15th century, the fortifications were improved in compliance with Captain Coëtquen's orders. At the end of the 16th century, during the League, the Duke of Mercœur modernised the ramparts, in light of new artillery techniques, and improved the area around the keep.

Today, fifteen towers and four gates still stand in the town. Unfortunately, the Brest Gate and part of the ramparts were destroyed in 1881 to improve access to the west side. After this very much contested initiative the ramparts became listed monuments.

The "castle" includes the keep, Coëtquen Tower and Guichet Gate. It also houses the town museum which recounts the history of Dinan and its surrounding area. At the end of the 14th century, Duke Jean IV ordered the construction of the keep for residential and defensive purposes. It now houses the museum's collections.

1.

2.

3.

4.

The 15th-century Coëtquen Tower features a large vaulted room on each of its three storeys. The lower room displays seven recumbent figures including one of Roland of Dinan. Starting at the castle, "Petits Fossés" walk leads past Connétable and Beaufort Towers. In the north west, "Grands Fossés" walk runs past St. Julien's Tower, Vaucouleurs Tower and the colossal Beaumanoir Tower near St. Malo Gate. From this point you can walk along the top of the ramparts as far as Rue Haute-Voie, passing above the Governor's Tower and Jerzual Gate. St. Catherine's Tower, opposite the viaduct, provides a wonderful view of the surrounding countryside with the river Rance and the old harbour down below. In the east, "Duchesse Anne" walk runs alongside the ramparts as far as Sillon Tower. Finally you reach Penthièvre Tower just before St. Louis Gate. This gate, which was constructed under Louis XIII, is the newest rampart gate and provides access to a delightful path leading down to the harbour.

Every even year in the summer, Dinan's local authorities organise the "Fête des Remparts" or rampart festival where scenes from daily life, tournaments, troubadours and processions recreate the town's former mediaeval atmosphere.

5.

"Place de l'Apport" square and surroundings

Between the castle and "Place de l'Apport" square, visitors cross the former "Place d'armes" square which now bears the name of Bertrand Du Guesclin, Constable of France. A beautiful equestrian statue depicts this warrior ready for battle. The statue was created by Emmanuel Frémiet, who also created Mont St. Michel's famous archangel. This square is lined with some beautiful 18th-century mansions.

Charming, half-timbered and corbelled houses line the old streets in the Apport district. The street names evoke the trades that made the town so prosperous, such as Rue de la Mittrie (coppersmiths), Rue de Larderie (meat sellers), Rue de la Ferronnerie (iron workers), Rue de la Lainerie (wool workers), Rue de la Poissonnerie (fishmongers), Rue de la Cordonnerie (cobblers) and Rue du Petit-Pain (bakers). The houses were mostly occupied by craftsmen and traders. On the ground floor, goods were displayed and customers received while the upper floors were used for storage or accommodation purposes. The "Maison de la Mère Pourcel" on "Place des Merciers" square bears traces of the weavers that once lived there, while the "Maison du Gisant" calls to mind the stone carver who once worked there. Hôtel Keratry, which blends so well into

2.

3.

1.

1.
The famous "Maison de la Mère Pourcel" on "Place des Merciers" square.

2.
Statue of Bertrand Du Guesclin on horseback.

3.
House with mullioned windows, Rue de l'Apport.

4.
Close-up of Hôtel Keratry.

4.

Rue de l'Horloge, did not actually originate in Dinan. Dinan's local authorities purchased the ruined building from the village of Lanvollon in 1930 before dismantling and painstakingly rebuilding it, stone by stone, in its present location in the town centre.

The 15th-century Clock Tower, or belfry, rises 60 metres above the town. The bell, a gift from Duchess Anne in 1507, would have been sounded by the town watchman in the event of fire or danger. This tower, a symbol of Dinan's powerful merchant class, housed the town hall up until the French Revolution. From the top of the belfry, the panoramic view extends over the many rooftops, streets and gardens, which in turn overlook the surrounding countryside.

5.

6.

5.
The belfry and Hôtel Keratry.

6.
The belfry or Clock Tower.

St. Saviour's Basilica and surroundings

The history of this church, which became a basilica in 1954, can be traced back to the crusades, when Rivallon Le Roux, Lord of Dinan, fought in Palestine. He made a vow to construct a church to the glory of God in his home town should he return home safely. After his return to Dinan, he fulfilled this vow. Some beautiful Romanesque elements remain from this period including the extremely beautiful south porch with its three arches, the baptismal font and the southern *longère* made up of six bays separated by tall columns.

The decoration has clearly been influenced by the East with its camels, lions and birds, etc. The church was extended in the 15th century to meet the requirements of a rapidly expanding population, and the building work was to take 150 years to complete. The nave was enlarged, the transept's two wings and side aisle were built and the chancel was added, together with its nine side-chapels, to give the church the appearance that we see today. The stained glass windows (1475-1525) were built at the same time as the side aisle; they depict the four apostles and four more saints: St. Mathurin, St. Armel, St. Yves and St. Brieuc. Parishioners saved the furnishings from destruction by vandals during the French Revolution. Admire the high altar, the various reredos and the "Our Lady of Virtues" bas-relief sent by St. Bonaventure

1.
The western façade
of St. Saviour's Basilica.

2.
The Basilica's apse viewed
from the English gardens.

1.

2.

L'Atelier
du
Bijou

Saint

3.

from Assisi to Henri d'Avaugour, founder of Cordeliers' Monastery. Bertrand Du Guesclin's cenotaph can also be found in this church.

The birthplace of the explorer and geographer, Auguste Pavie, stands on "Place Saint-Sauveur" square and is one of the oldest buildings in the area. In the 19th century, the English gardens replaced the parish cemetery behind the church's apse. From above the ramparts, between St. Catherine's Tower and Cardinal Tower, you can admire the wonderful view of the old harbour, the Rance valley and the surrounding countryside. Auguste Pavie's bust can be seen in this garden.

In Rue Waldeck-Rousseau, Dinan's local authorities have opened the CREC, a trade and culture centre, in an old monastery. The centre boasts a library with a multimedia section, the "Kiosque" music school and a conference centre with an auditorium and exhibition areas.

Next to the CREC, the chapel of the Catherinettes' Convent (and in particular its entrance) is a typical example of Counter-Reformation architecture. Inside, there is a *trompe l'oeil* reredos and the ceiling above the chancel is decorated with frescoes.

3.
Entrance to St. Saviour's Basilica.

4.
The English gardens.

4.

1.

St. Malo's Church and surroundings

The original St. Malo's Church was built in the 11th century on the site where St. Joachim's Chapel now stands. The ramparts were built leaving the church standing outside and so it was destroyed to prevent the enemy from using it as a hiding place. In the late 15th century, Jean de Rohan built the current church inside the ramparts. The chancel and transept are wonderful examples of flamboyant Gothic architecture. The Wars of Religion interrupted the work for a while. In 1620, the entrance was completed. The French Revolution was a dark time for the unfinished building. It was vandalised and pillaged and was not restored as a place of worship until 1803. The nave was finally completed under Napoleon III in fine 15th-century style. The outside of the eastern section of the building abounds with arch-buttresses and gargoyles but the church tower was never actually given a steeple. The dark, and slender interior is conducive to meditation and spiritual elevation.

The church's outstanding early 20th-century stained glass windows depict scenes from the lives of famous laymen who supported the religious cause. For instance, Anne of Brittany is depicted entering the town by the Brest Gate on her visit to Dinan in 1505, and Grignion de Monfort is illustrated visiting Count and Countess de La Garaye, who helped the poor and sick. The organs, built by the English organ builder, Oldknow, were installed in 1889. Their blue and gold painted pipes are of rare elegance. At the base of the nave, two stoups welcome believers. One of them was created in the 15th century and was doubtless used as a baptismal font and the second, modern, one depicts a devil grimacing beneath the weight of the holy water! As you leave the church, note the shells and urns decorating the Renaissance entrance.

Grande Rue leads to "Place Duclos" square, built on the site of the old Brest Gate. The statue of Jehan De Beaumanoir, Bertrand Du Guesclin's companion, can be seen in this square. In 1357, De Beaumanoir fought in the "Battle of the Thirty" near Josselin. Wounded by the English and almost dying of thirst, he begged for a drink. His cousin Geoffroy de Blois responded with this famous quote: "Drink your own blood, Beaumanoir, and your thirst will be quenched." This statue, created in 1910, depicts this warrior standing sword in hand, ready for battle.

1.
St. Malo's Church and apse.

2.
The Governor's house.

3.
Dinan harbour.

2.

The old Cordeliers' Monastery, now converted into a private school, stands on the other side of the church. The monastery was originally built in the 13th century but its main door, cloisters (of which only the deambulatory remains), main twin-turreted courtyard and former Cordelier monk refectory were added in the 15th century. The States of Brittany held meetings on several occasions in the chapter house which has since been converted into a refectory.

3.

Rue du Jerzual and the old harbour

Rue du Jerzual, which continues into Rue du Petit-Fort on the other side of the gate, is doubtless the town's most picturesque street. Until the viaduct was built in 1852, these two streets provided the only access to the town centre from the harbour. Try to imagine the hustle and bustle as travellers and merchants climbed up and down this long and dangerously steep cobbled street. Admire the lovely façades of the beautiful half-timbered houses on either side of the street. The largest among them is the Governor's house in Rue du Petit-Fort, which was built between 1620 and 1650. This four-storey building extends back a long way and is a fine example of a property owned by the prosperous traders that made up the town's wealthy class. Further down, near the harbour, former tanners' houses can be recognised by their large bay windows on the upper floors where leather, delivered by river transport, was laid out to dry. The town's merchants and traders have now been replaced by tourists who struggle up and down this street (which is still as steep as ever) where artists and craftsmen continue to display their creations.

The harbour has preserved all its charm. Leisure boats and ferries packed with tourists from St. Malo or Dinard have replaced the river's trading activities. Passers-by can stop for a refreshing break on a café or restaurant terrace, looking out onto the old bridge, viaduct and peaceful river Rance.

The "Maison de la Grande Vigne" is located at the end of the quayside heading in the Taden direction.
This property was owned by the late artist Yvonne Jean-Haffen. Climb the small rickety staircase to explore this artist's house which is open to the public. The towpath, running past the building, leads to Taden and is one of many countryside walks around Dinan that tourists can enjoy.

The "Maison de la Rance" has been set up in an old converted farmhouse on the other side of the river, opposite the harbour. This nature centre welcomes nature and history lovers and describes life along the river bank. It also describes the geomorphology of the river Rance and its surrounding natural environment. Nature outings are organised to further your understanding of this river environment which constantly changes with the seasons.

1.

1.
Quayside and old houses lining the harbour.

2.
Half-timbered house in Rue du Jerzual.

2.

3.

4.

Famous Dinan personalities

Bertrand Du Guesclin (1320-1380)

Born south-west of Dinan, Du Guesclin had an aggressive nature and, already as a teenager, stood out at regional tournaments. At 34 years old, after a victory against the English, he was knighted by Charles de Blois. During the War of Succession, he sided with the King of France. In 1370, Charles V made him Constable of France, i.e. Commander-in-Chief of the Army. In 1380, he died in combat, far from his native Brittany. All his life, he fought to drive the English out of France. As well as the statue of him on horseback, Dinan has several other souvenirs of its *enfant terrible,* such as his heart, which, as per his wishes, is kept in St. Saviour's Basilica in Dinan.

Count de La Garaye (1675-1755)

After a carefree and unruly youth, and following the death of his brother and nephew, Claude Toussaint Marot became Count de La Garaye. At 35 years old he suddenly found himself in charge of a large and wealthy estate: the Plouër hotel in Dinan, the "Grand-Cour" manor in Taden and the majestic "Chateau de La Garaye" north-west of Dinan. He became aware of the poverty around him and, with the help of his wife, increased his medical and surgical knowledge and opened a hospital in the buildings surrounding his castle. In 1731, his reputation reached the court of King Louis XV, who encouraged him and published his research results on “essential salts”. As requested, he was not buried in the family vault in St. Malo's Church, but with the poor in Taden's lowly cemetery. In Dinan, a street is named after him and, in St. Malo's Church, a stained-glass window depicts him in his castle, surrounded by the destitute he strove to help.

5.

3.
Close-up of a house in Rue du Jerzual.

4.
Close-up of cobbles in Rue du Jerzual.

5.
Duclos-Pinot's bust along the "Petits Fossés" walk.

Charles Duclos-Pinot (1704-1772)

By the time he finished his education which he began in his home town, continued in Rennes and finally ended in Paris, Duclos-Pinot was moving in literary circles. He is remembered, above all, as a libertine, man of letters and King Louis XV's historiographer. This academic was Mayor of Dinan from 1744 to 1749. He built the "Grands Fossés" and "Petits Fossés" walks where his bust, created in 1836 by Jean Duseigneur, is on display.

Auguste Pavie (1847-1925)

What a fabulous destiny this young man from Dinan had! He started out as a 5th-class mail clerk in Cambodia, then went on to become an explorer, geographer, diplomat and even Consul General of Laos! He was a gentle man who spent twenty-five years in the Far-East, where he was nicknamed "the bare handed conqueror". When he came back to Brittany, he wrote several works, including ten volumes of the *Mission Pavie: Indochine 1879-1895.* This man of rare intelligence liked to say: "I have known the joy of being loved by the people whom I visited". In Dinan, you can visit his birthplace in "Place Saint-Sauver" square and also see his bust in the English gardens.

1.

Théodore Botrel (1868-1925)

"Théodore Botrel, Breton bard and singer, was born here" is inscribed on his house in Rue de la Mittrie in Dinan's old quarters. After trying his hand at various trades, he started a career as a singer and is now known throughout all French-speaking countries. His songs about Breton life, which he performed in traditional costume, bore witness to the Breton lifestyle of faith and hard work. His song *La Paimpolaise* is one of the most famous in his repertoire.

2.

Roger Vercel (1894-1957)

Born in Le Mans, Vercel was appointed as a French teacher at Dinan secondary school in 1920 and was to live in the town for the rest of his life. He wrote a biography of Du Guesclin and many other novels which are set either in Brittany or at sea. Several of these novels were made into films, such as *Remorque* and *Capitaine Conan.* He received the Prix Goncourt in 1934. A street is named after him in the town he loved to live and write in and, in Rue de Léhon, a plaque on his house evokes his attachment to Dinan.

Yvonne Jean-Haffen (1925-1993)

This Parisian was passionate about drawing. In 1925 she met Mathurin Méheut, a Breton who became her mentor and friend. A year later, he introduced her to Brittany and the following year she bought a house on the hillside, at the far end of Dinan harbour. The "Grande Vigne" became her studio, where she often invited Méheut, as well as other artists, writers and poets. She travelled throughout Brittany, which inspired her to draw many scenes, such as religious heritage, rural life and fishing scenes. It seems as if nothing escaped her eye. She compiled her drawings of sacred fountains in a book and in 1972 created the Mathurin-Méheut museum in Lamballe. At the end of her life, she donated her house and artwork to the town of Dinan. The property is open to the public in high season and the lower cottage, which is nicknamed "Vignette", welcomes painters from France and abroad, inspired by Dinan and its region.

3.

1. Auguste Pavie's bust in the English Gardens.

2. The "Grande Vigne", artist Yvonne Jean-Haffen's house.

3. Théodore Botrel in Breton costume. (Cartopole de Baud)

5.

4.
Taden: "Grand-Cour" manor.

5.
Léhon: castle ruins.

6.
Léhon: the abbey church.

7.
The "Chateau de La Garaye" ruins.

6.

7.

Around Dinan

Léhon

Bordering the Rance to the south of Dinan, Léhon has long maintained its charm and tranquillity. The ruins of the 11th-century feudal castle, which, in the past, defended the Rance and Dinan against invaders, are still visible. St. Magloire's Priory, built by monks in the 9th century, stands between Pont aux Ânes bridge and the many well preserved old houses, on land donated by Nominoé, the King of Brittany. The area prospered up to the arrival of the Normans. The abbey was rebuilt and extended. During the French Revolution, it served as an army store and tannery. In 1897 the church was turned back into a place of worship. You can still see the recumbent statues of the Beaumanoir family as well as the cloister and old refectory. The priory's old press-house is home to the town hall.

Taden

Situated on the edge of the river Rance, this village still features traces of the Gallo-Roman occupation. Taden was once a very busy harbour. The 14th-century "Grand-Cour" manor is one of the region's few gatehouses which still has its watchtower. The church, built in the same period, contains the tomb of the Count and Countess de La Garaye.

La Garaye Castle

At the exit of Dinan, in the direction of Ploubalay, are the ruins of the Count de La Garaye's Renaissance castle. The Count built a hospice here which also served to teach medicine to young students. In the 19th century, the ruins inspired many romantic artists. The elegant stairway turret has preserved its fine allure and the outbuildings, which served to house the sick, are still there today.

Useful information

Tourist Information Centre,
Rue du Château
Tel.: +33 (0)2 96 87 69 76

Market: Thursdays
("Place Du Guesclin" and "Place du Champ" squares)

Dinan Castle and Museum
Tel.: +33 (0)2 96 39 45 20

Clock Tower
Rue de l'Horloge
Tel.: +33 (0)2 96 87 02 26

"Maison d'artiste de la Grande Vigne"
103, Rue du Quai
Tel.: +33 (0)2 96 87 90 80

"Maison de la Rance"
Talard Quayside in Lanvallay.
Tel.: +33 (0)2 96 87 00 40

Léhon Abbey
Tel.: +33 (0)2 96 87 69 76/+33 (0)2 96 87 40 40

Special thanks
to Marie-Hélène Ledan
for her invaluable help

1.

2.

1.
Close-up of the apse on St. Saviour's Basilica.

2.
Rue du Jerzual.

3.
Shop signs in Rue de la Cordonnerie.

Captions on panoramic poster:
The river Rance seen from the viaduct which links Dinan to Lanvallay.

Rue du Jerzual.

House adorned with flowers in Rue du Petit-Fort.

Saint Michel, nicknamed "Saint Dinan" (Mère Pourcel's house).

3.